Having Someone W...
Barriers to change in the public care of children

Jenny Morris

SUPPORTED BY
JR
JOSEPH
ROWNTREE
FOUNDATION

NATIONAL CHILDREN'S BUREAU

The National Children's Bureau (NCB) works to identify and promote the well-being and interests of all children and young people across every aspect of their lives.

It encourages professionals and policy makers to see the needs of the whole child and emphasises the importance of multidisciplinary, cross-agency partnerships. The NCB has adopted and works within the UN Convention on the Rights of the Child.

It collects and disseminates information about children and promotes good practice in children's services through research, policy and practice development, membership, publications, conferences, training and an extensive library and information service.

Several Councils and Fora are based at the NCB and contribute significantly to the breadth of its influence. It also works in partnership with Children in Scotland and Children in Wales and other voluntary organisations concerned for children and their families.

The **Joseph Rowntree Foundation** has supported this project as part of its programme of research and innovative development projects, which it hopes will be of value to policy makers and practitioners.

The views expressed in this book are those of the authors and not necessarily those of the National Children's Bureau or the Joseph Rowntree Foundation.

© National Children's Bureau and Joseph Rowntree Foundation, 2000

All rights reserved. No part of this publication may be reproduced, stored in a retrieval system or transmitted in any form by any person without the written permission of the publisher.

ISBN 1 900990 56 3

Published by National Children's Bureau Enterprises Ltd, 8 Wakley Street, London EC1V 7QE

National Children's Bureau Enterprises Ltd is the trading company for the National Children's Bureau (Registered Charity number 258825).

Typeset by LaserScript Ltd, Mitcham, Surrey CR4 4NA

Printed and bound in the United Kingdom by Redwood Books, Trowbridge, Wiltshire BA14 8RN

Contents

Preface	iv
1 What gets in the way of change?	1
2 What helps to bring about change for the better?	28
Conclusion	57
Bibliography	59

Preface

In 1999, the Joseph Rowntree Foundation commissioned me to write a 'think piece' – in other words, a short report which seeks to get people thinking. Therefore, this is not a piece of research. Neither is it a review of how the public care system currently fails children, although a lot of the research concerning this is referred to in this report. Instead, I have attempted to address the question of what gets in the way of changing things for children in the public care system. Given that we now know that things often go wrong for looked after children, why haven't central and local government, the child care organisations and the social work profession been able to do better for them? This is an enormous issue and the aim here is to get people thinking about it, rather than provide a comprehensive answer.

The starting point for the report was a seminar organised by the Joseph Rowntree Foundation in the autumn of 1998, attended by people from the main voluntary sector organisations concerned with looked after children and by prominent researchers in the field. At that meeting four key areas were identified:

- involving and listening to children and young people, from individual assessments to the strategic planning of services;
- the role of needs-led assessments and a needs-led approach to the commissioning and delivery of services;
- the training implications of promoting models of good practice, ranging from front-line workers through to senior management;
- the changing policy environment, including the promotion of effective inter-agency and inter-departmental working.

The current report builds on this discussion and also on interviews held, during the summer of 1999, with:

- five groups of children and young people who are or have been looked after (35 children and young people);
- people who hold or have held senior positions in the child care field with a vision for change;
- people (at senior management and front-line level) who are currently involved in bringing about change.

Those consulted were not, of course, representative of people working in the care system or of looked after children and young people. Nevertheless, some common themes emerged from our discussions and these are used to structure the report. I asked those I spoke to for permission to use their words to illustrate the key issues and these quotations are used throughout the report. Some quotes are used anonymously or with pseudonyms while others are fully attributed, according to people's wishes.

The background to this report is both what we know already about children in the public care system, and the various policy initiatives of the current government. One way of presenting what we know about how the care system fails children is to focus on the very negative outcomes for many looked after children. These have been summarised, for example, as follows:

'Compared with children in general, children who need the care of public authorities are up to ten times more likely to be excluded from school, 12 times more likely to leave school with no qualifications, four times more likely to be unemployed, 60 times more likely to join the ranks of the young homeless, 50 times more likely to be sent to prison and four times more likely to suffer from mental health problems. In addition, their own children are up to 66 times more likely to need public care than the children of those who have not been in public care themselves.'

(UK Joint Working Party on Foster Care, 1999, p. 6)

However, another way of looking at it is to focus on the characteristics of the care system itself, the factors which create barriers to looked after children having a good quality of life. Research tells us that the care system in the 1990s often fails children in that:

- Children in care usually experience a number of different changes of placement (Biehal and others, 1995; Millham, Bullock and Hosie, 1986).
- Social services departments often do not provide adequate or appropriate support to enable looked after children to have helpful experiences of contact with their families (BAAF, 1995).
- Residential care can provide stability and other advantages, but many residential units fail to offer children secure relationships and therefore inhibit their emotional development (Bullock, Little and Millham, 1993).
- The care and education systems in general are failing to promote the educational potential of children who are looked after (Social Services Inspectorate and Office for Standards in Education, 1995, p. 3).
- Children are now more likely to attend review meetings, but they are not fully involved or consulted in decisions about their care (Sinclair and Grimshaw, 1997).
- Disabled children are often not accorded the full protection of the 1989 Children Act regulations and it is very common for social workers to fail to 'ascertain the wishes and feelings' of disabled children when carrying out assessments and reviews of placements (Social Services Inspectorate, 1998a; Morris, 1998b).
- Children's homes and local authorities often fail to acknowledge or meet the needs of black and minority ethnic children (Social Services Inspectorate, 1993, p. vi).

Perhaps one of the most damning findings from research is that from one of the very few studies of children's own opinions of the care system. The Who Cares? Trust's survey of looked after children found that, when asked to select from a range of possible responses to the question 'What is the best thing about being in care?', only 21 per cent of them ticked 'Having someone who cares' (Shaw, 1998, p. 56).

Jenny Morris
January 2000

1 What gets in the way of change?

Introduction

This section of the report is divided up into the topics that were raised when people were asked: 'What gets in the way of change?' The nature of the question resulted in people highlighting their criticisms of the current system. This section therefore inevitably contains a lot of negative messages and may seem unfair to those who are trying their hardest, in difficult circumstances, to deliver a good service to looked after children. Nevertheless, the same themes were raised again and again – by young people, front-line workers and senior managers. They are presented here in an attempt to highlight the reality of what gets in the way of bringing about positive change.

Many of the barriers to change concern people and the way they behave. This is an inevitable part of a human rights perspective: an emphasis on the rights of individual human beings means that we have to confront the actions of all of us as human beings and how we might be contravening or promoting the rights of others.

Public attitudes to children

'The media always put down young people, not just us young people in care but all young people.'
Derek Sewell

'Public attitudes toward children affect every level of all organisations and everybody. The common assumption is that children belong to their parents, that they are property or chattels, and that parents have the same rights over them as they do towards other things that they own. It is really quite difficult to convey that these are individual human beings with rights of their own and that parental responsibilities towards them are at least as important as any rights they might have over them.'

Sir William Utting

Perhaps the biggest barrier that social services departments and all those working with looked after children have to contend with is the social attitudes towards children in general.

'We have all been conditioned by a culture in which deliberately hurting children is still accepted both socially and legally, in which concepts of adult 'ownership' of children, who should be 'seen and not heard' persist.'
(Gulbenkian Foundation, 1993, p. xv)

These public attitudes can get in the way, not only of protecting children from harm, but also of recognising some forms of adult behaviour as abusive. Generally, it is not considered acceptable for one adult to hit another, to restrict their liberty, constantly to criticise them or to allow them no privacy. Yet adults, in their various roles of looking after children, are often considered to be entitled to behave in these ways towards children – and sometimes it is even considered to be in a child's interests to do so.

Other aspects of the attitude of the general public towards children can get in the way of them having any opportunity to make their feelings known about their experiences. Children are considered to be inconsistent (they change their minds), untrustworthy (they make things up) and, because they lack the experience of age, unable to make valid judgements (they don't know what they're talking about). These attitudes undermine the requirement placed on social workers by the 1989 Children Act to consult with and involve children in decisions about their care. They can also undermine attempts to involve children and young people collectively in the development of policy and services.

'People have found it very difficult to take on board the idea of children being involved in the service user participation strategy. They said things like children and young people don't really know what the issues are, they change their minds, children often make complaints but there's no substance to them, they're not consistent, they might find it difficult to attend meetings. And I'm saying, we all find it difficult to attend meetings, can't we do this in a different way? We need to challenge the idea that adults have the monopoly on making good decisions.'

Linda Marshall, Children's Rights Adviser, Essex Social Services

Public attitudes to children in care

In addition to social attitudes towards children in general, attitudes towards children in care in particular can get in the way of promoting their interests. The status itself can undermine children's well-being in that there is a stigma attached to being in care. While there is public concern about child abuse and neglect, there is often a failure to link this concern with children in care – in spite of the fact that many of these children are in care precisely because of abuse or neglect. Instead, there is a common labelling of children in the care system as 'mad or bad'.

'If there was one thing I could change it would the attitudes of our neighbours, for them to think that kids in children's homes aren't that bad.'

Carly Cox

'The teacher said, 'If you start bringing in drugs, you'll be expelled'. And I thought I'm in care because of what happened to me. But he just assumed it was my fault.'

Cheryl

'There's great prejudice that if you're in care, it's your fault. You could be beaten black and blue and social services move you out just to keep you safe, but it's your fault. ... I started talking to the taxi driver about the meeting I was going to [part of a literacy week for looked after children] and I mentioned the words 'in care' and he said, 'Oh, you mean delinquent kids, don't you?''

John Kohlasch

'What people forget is, when they get a paper in the morning and it says, child has been raped, child has been abused and they think oh, my God, that's really out of order, and then when it comes to children's homes, they forget that's probably why they're in a children's home and they automatically think those children are bad. But half of us are in there, not through our fault, but through the fault of other people.'

Kay Connolly

'Everyone thinks you're a no-hoper when you're in care.'

Stephanie

The human rights of children are often not the dominant value base of social services departments

'It's almost as if children and young people are like objects. We don't have a say in what's happening. We're just on the receiving end of budgets and things like that.'

Tommy Turner

'If you're operating in a political situation where as a Director of Social Services the Social Services Committee is going to sack you if you go over budget, no questions asked, and that's at the top of the list, you're likely to produce an organisation in which mechanistic values take over.'

Sir William Utting

'By 1997, Ealing's Social Services Department had a structure and culture which wasn't in touch with the social work process. Throughout the 1980s and into the 1990s, there had been a push to move into a business-type culture which, although there were positive things about that, also meant that managers seemed to lose sight of what the social work process was about.'

John Skinner, Assistant Director (Children and Families), London Borough of Ealing

The UN Convention on the Rights of the Child has provided an important moral framework for the duties of social services departments under the Children Act. However, during the 1980s and early 1990s, this moral framework often lost out to more dominant values: those associated with an emphasis on business efficiency. Social services departments were required by central government during the 1980s and first half of the 1990s to be more efficient and to adopt an approach to the delivery of services which relied on costing assessments and services, and creating internal markets. There was also an assumption that good management in the public sector was no different from good management in the private sector.

When a social services department focuses more on the cost of doing an assessment than on what goes on in the assessment, it is probably inevitable that the quality of social work will suffer. If managers have inadequate social work knowledge and skills to promote and nurture good practice, then the quality of work with children and families will certainly be undermined.

'It feels as if our management just don't understand what 'working with children and families' is about. All they're interested in is budgets, bed-spaces, how many assessments you've done. You know, you have to build up a relationship with these kids in order to have any impact. But we've got no time for that and, anyway, it's not what our managers are interested in.'

Social worker in a town in the North-East of England

The concept of 'being a good parent' is not one that social services authorities have generally applied to their own relationships with looked after children

The succession of child abuse scandals, the greater public awareness of abuse and the public criticism of social workers has, not surprisingly, resulted in social services departments focusing very strongly on the protection of children from harm. Some people feel, however, that this has taken attention away from social services' ongoing role of looking after children whose families cannot do so. The Who Cares? Trust argues:

'The current focus of public care is on the protection of the child, with relatively little attention being given to the roles of nurturer and educator – roles which we would expect of a 'good parent'. This prevents the provision of a service which takes a holistic approach to a child's development based on his or her real needs.'

(The Who Cares? Trust, 1998, p. 1)

'The aim for the local authority should be how to be a good, aspiring, effective parent. However, the local authority doesn't apply these parenting aims to the education of its children. As a good parent you have to get them to school, you have to know what they're good at, what their problems are, and as an everyday parent you have to have some sense of continuity about the child's history – what's worked for them in the past, what hasn't. And local authorities have never accepted this task. Yet from the child's point of view, they are totally dependent on the local authority to get for them out of the education system what other parents want for their kids.'

Barbara Fletcher, Education Policy Officer,
Local Government Association

The organisation as a whole needs to care about what happens to each individual child, whether they are happy, whether they are doing well at school, whether they are healthy, whether they have friends, and so on. In reality, the responsibility for children's welfare is fragmented amongst different people, different organisations, and those who are in the closest contact with looked after children – foster carers and residential care workers – are probably the most undervalued part of the whole structure in that they receive low pay, little training, and often have generally poor working conditions.

Responses to children's needs are often dominated by a service-led approach

> 'I was put in this short-term placement and I stayed nine months and I didn't want to leave by then. And they said they wanted to keep me. But my social worker said, 'No, that's a short-term placement, we have to find you a long-term placement.''
>
> Ray Jackson

If social services departments are to do their best for each child for whom they are responsible, those making decisions about substitute care will have to be able to respond to a particular child's needs. This can be blocked by:

- Strongly-held views about what is the best course of action: as Roy Parker pointed out in his review of residential care for children in 1988, 'The pursuit of what is generally considered to be good for children (or good for children in care) has to be tested repeatedly against the question 'what is good for *this* child?' (Parker, 1988, p. 114).
- The way services are organised can get in the way of responding to a particular child's needs in a particular circumstance: the example most commonly raised by those consulted for this report was where a child had been placed with short-term foster carers but had settled down well, wanted to remain in the placement and the carers wanted him to stay. The funding and organisation of foster care – the separation of foster care placements into short-term and long-term provision

– usually prevented this being possible. This type of experience has also been highlighted by Voice for the Child in Care (1998) in their advocacy work with looked after children and young people.
- Children's experiences of substitute care are inevitably determined by whether there are adequate levels of services available. If a social services department does not have enough foster carers or cannot find or pay for residential placements that meet the needs of a particular child, then it is inevitable that responses will be dominated by service considerations rather than what the child needs. This is such a crucial factor working against a needs-led approach to looked after children that it is worth separating out the problems with the supply of residential and foster care as two separate issues (see the next two points).

Jackson and Thomas's review of what helps to create stability for looked after children concluded that:

'It is quite clear from the evidence that some children are being subjected to almost continuous change in their living arrangements for which there is no possible justification and which is utterly destructive of their well-being, development and chances of forming relationships.'

(Jackson and Thomas, 1999, p. 39)

'Before social workers decide to put you in a placement I think you should have contact with that placement beforehand, see if it's going to work out properly and everything. Because before I went to the kids' home, in six months I've moved eight, nine times and nothing worked out really. In the end I went to The Mead, then I was put in another placement. I had no contact beforehand, it went totally wrong, I went back to The Mead. They need to build up a relationship before they put you in a placement, so that you know how the household works, to know the rules, to have a say, to see how it goes.'

Melanie Brooker

> 'I've been moved about six times, in about three years. It would be nice if they'd ask you what sort of place you'd like, not sort of say you'll go there. Ask you what things you like, what you like doing. They don't even give you an option, they just ship you off somewhere. And it's what they think, not what you think.'
>
> John Dalley

> 'It's about whether it's cheaper for them, whether they've got enough money, whether a place is costing too much.'
>
> Danny Carter

There are not enough foster carers and not enough recognition given to the skills required

David Berridge's review of research on foster care concluded that:

'there has generally been a significant shortage of foster carers. It has often not been possible to place children in the type of environment that was being sought and, instead, compromises have had to be made.'

(Berridge, 1997, p. 76)

Foster care continues to be under-resourced and the majority of foster carers receive no financial reward for the work they do:

'The traditional voluntary basis of foster care has meant that carers continue to be considered as providing services outside formal professional child care structures – and many carers report feeling under-valued, unsupported and unable to contribute effectively to the decision-making processes which affect the children for whom they care.'

(UK Joint Working Party on Foster Care, 1999, p. 6)

> 'There's hardly any foster carers out there, and no wonder the way social workers treat them sometimes. It's just the attitude towards them, it's like they're nothing. My social worker really put my

foster carer down. They're not going to get foster carers if they treat them like that. They've got the attitude that they know best, we've got our university degrees, we're better than you.'
Melanie Brooker

'They need more foster homes because there's loads of children bunged up in one kids' home.'
Danny Carter

There are particular barriers to developing foster care services for disabled children and black and minority ethnic children. A failure to address, or sometimes even to recognise, the nature of these barriers, means that disabled children and black children are more likely to be placed in residential care. There is a particular need to recruit foster carers from the black community.

'The black community here in Liverpool have historically only experienced statutory services in a negative way – whether it's police services or over-zealous social workers. So to think that without much effort – and there hasn't been much effort – you could turn that well-bred belief around so that they get some trust and think 'I can work well with an agency, they will respect and value me, so I'll give fostering a go' – it's just unrealistic.'
Melanie McGuinness, Manager, Black Residential Child Care Support Team

There is an inadequate pool of good residential (including specialist) provision to enable local authorities to make appropriate placement decisions for children who would benefit from residential care

The government's review of safeguards for children living away from home concluded that 'residential child care as a national service has shrunk to below that which provides a reasonable choice for children' (Utting, 1997, p. 21). The earlier Utting review of residential child care had identified a continuing role for children's homes, emphasising that 'residential care should be a positive, joint choice' (Utting, 1991, p. 62). However, almost a decade later, this is not what it feels like for many young people. Nor is it the experience of many residential care workers.

> 'I did actually run to my social worker and she just didn't give two hoots and she just put me in a place I didn't want to be. Because she reckoned there wasn't enough room in any other places. I had to run away from there, just for people to listen to me.'
>
> John Dalley

> 'We just get children dumped on us, usually at very short notice. It's very difficult to see how we can be part of a service 'targeted on the need of the individual child', which is what they say we're supposed to be. Basically, children end up with us because there's nowhere else for them to go.'
>
> Residential care manager, London Borough

The House of Commons Select Committee on Health received not only evidence of the continuing valuable role of children's homes, but also the problems caused by the reduction in their number:

- Social workers often have no choice or flexibility about making placements.
- Some children's homes contain an inappropriate mix of children (in terms of age, gender, needs and behaviour), leading to very difficult experiences for individual children.
- Specialist provision often has to be purchased outside a local authority's area, leading to children being placed many miles from their family and community.
- There is a large variation between local authorities in the amount of residential care provided by them.

(House of Commons Select Committee on Health, 1998)

Social workers are often not able to fulfil the role that looked after children want from them

Almost all the children and young people consulted for the purpose of this report said, unprompted, that they wanted to see their social worker more often. Many of them said that social workers didn't have enough time for them, that their caseloads were too high and that, when they did see their social worker, they felt that they weren't being listened to.

'She only comes to see me once every two months. She doesn't want to know how I'm getting on.'

Karl Hurding

'I just wish my social worker would come and see me. He hasn't seen me since my review.'

Anthony Hillern

'All we want social workers to do is be there when we need them.'

Derek Sewell

'I just think they should see you more. My foster carer was really ill for a long time, and social services never bothered with us. My foster carer had cancer and they never bothered to come and see us. It was just as she was passing away that I got, 'Oh, I'm so sorry' and I thought, 'I don't want to know you'. It was only right at the end that they showed interest so I don't want to know her any more.'

Rachel Smith

Discussions were held with two groups of social workers, one in a London borough, the other in a town in the north-east of England. The social workers expressed the same kinds of criticisms of what they were able to do as did the children and young people. They felt their caseloads were too high to give children the individual attention and time they needed; they said there was barely enough time to fulfil their statutory duties in terms of carrying out reviews, filling in Looked After Children (LAC) forms, and arranging alternatives when placements broke down.

'I always feel that there are other things I should be doing. I'm juggling which child has priority and in the back of my mind all the time is the worry that the situations I don't put the time into could collapse.'
Social worker in a London borough

'There's not the time to do the kind of things that I thought I would be doing when I thought about coming into social work with children. When I was training there was time to take a child out, go swimming with them, talk to them about their day at school. But now I'm lucky if I get to see each of my case-load for 20 minutes every two months or so. One of them said to me the other day, every time I ring you, you're on duty, or out on a visit, or on an emergency call, or off sick, or on holiday. And that just made me feel dreadful.'
Social worker in a town in the north-east of England

Not enough emphasis is put on the inter-personal and communication skills needed by social workers and other child care workers

'Probably the two most important things about social work are inter-personal skills and communication. And I have to say that those are the two things that I think we do worst as a business.'
John Skinner, Assistant Director (Children and Families), London Borough of Ealing

While it is recognised that social workers have developed new skills and expertise in assessing and evaluating the risk of abuse, concern has been raised by many that the standards of skills and expertise required for longer-term work with children, the support required for successful adoption or fostering placements and the involvement of children in decisions about their care, are not as high as they should be (Social Services Inspectorate 1996, 1998b, 1999a, 1999b).

Recent evaluation of training for residential child care managers indicates that not enough emphasis has been placed on communication skills. When communication skills did figure in the training, they usually focused on younger children rather than adolescents, who are the largest group in residential care (Hills and Child, 1998).

'When I first moved in, I was left in my room to unpack. And I stayed there for the evening, I didn't come down. I was 13, it was two days after my birthday. They should have come up and helped me and talked to me, but they went downstairs, they don't care.'

David Pearce

Some people who work with children don't like children. They disempower them and, at worst, abuse them

'Staff who work in children's homes should treat us with the same amount of respect as they'd like to be treated themselves. They think they own you. They don't treat us with respect but they still expect us to treat them with respect.'

Kurtis Hall

People who work in residential homes, who were consulted for the purposes of this report, identified that one of the major barriers to change is the existence, in some residential services, of a core group of staff (sometimes including senior management) who have been in post for a long period of time, and who are used to relating to children in a way which does not recognise their human rights. In this kind of situation, it can be very difficult for new members of staff to resist oppressive practices, particularly when they feel that 'whistle blower' policies do not offer sufficient protection and the whole culture of the workplace undermines their faith in their own judgement about what is wrong.

'There's a core of residential workers in our area, who've been there for years. It's a culture that's grown up, it's about power. They've got the power and the kids haven't. And if you want to do something about it, you stand alone.'

Social worker in a town in the north-east of England

'The attitude towards these kids is 'They're fucking bastards' and 'I'm going to show you and I've got the keys and I'm in charge and you do what I say because I'm in control and I'm an adult.' And 'Why do you think you're here in the first place? Because nobody wants you.' And it's very difficult for someone like me. I've been there three and a half months, I'm a single parent, I need my job. There isn't anyone for me to go to, unless I want to lose my job. They all stick up for each other, cover for each other.'

Residential care worker

Services are not very good at addressing all aspects of children's needs and identities

The corporate parent needs to address all the disadvantages that looked after children may experience, in the way that a good parent would try to help a child who experienced racism, sexism, heterosexism or prejudice against them because of impairment or appearance.

Issues of ethnicity, cultural identity and combating racism cannot be satisfactorily addressed without adequate training and understanding amongst staff, and resources put into recruiting social workers and carers from local minority ethnic communities. The evidence is, however, that this does not always happen and that many black and minority ethnic children remain poorly served by the care system (Barn, Sinclair and Ferdinand, 1997; Ince, 1998).

'The staff at the children's home didn't understand about what I needed to look after my skin and things. I felt like an alien, you know?'

Shirley Watson

'I had this white guy for my social worker and he just didn't have a clue that I just couldn't talk to him about what had happened to me. Maybe I could now I'm older and I've been through the care system but at that time, I mean, I was a ten-year-old Asian girl, I couldn't talk to strangers, let alone a guy like that.'

Mira

Like black children, disabled children account for a disproportionate number of looked after children and are more likely to be in residential settings than in foster placements. The SSI Inspection of services to disabled children and their families concluded that many social services staff have only a limited understanding of equal opportunities issues relating to disabled children and young people (Social Services Inspectorate, 1998a, p. 3).

'The biggest barrier is that disabled children aren't valued and the same standards of care aren't applied to them as to non-disabled children.'
Karen Castle, Children's Commissioning Manager, London Borough of Newham

Some disabled children become 'fully accommodated' because of a lack of local resources which would have enabled their families to look after them at home. In some circumstances, disabled children are accommodated in residential schools and their looked after status is not recognised (Morris, 1998b). Disabled children are also particularly vulnerable to not being consulted in decisions about their care.

'I repeatedly got forms from social workers doing assessments or reviews of disabled children with 'not applicable' under the heading 'Child's views'. I sent them back, pointing out to the social worker that this isn't good enough.'
Service Manager (Disabled Children), Social Services Department, County Council

There is a dearth of information which would help to address equalities issues for looked after children and young people.

There are few research studies which focus specifically on the experiences of black and minority ethnic children, disabled children or on young gay men and lesbians who are looked after. At the same time, research concerning looked after children in general rarely pays particular attention to these issues. Moreover, social services departments do not gather information which would help highlight these experiences. As a result, policies, procedures and practices are developed without paying attention to the needs of particular groups of children and the nature of the support they require (Bains, 1999, p. 4).

There isn't enough attention paid to listening to children

Although the UN Convention on the Rights of the Child and the 1989 Children Act insist that children have the right to be consulted, there is still evidence that those working with children in public care do not listen enough to what they have to say. Research indicates that children and young people are now more likely to attend review meetings, but that barriers to their proper involvement include:

- The environment and the number of people attending reviews can be intimidating.
- Relevant documentation is often not shared with the child or young person.
- Children or young people are inadequately prepared for reviews and thus experience difficulties in participating.

(Sinclair and Grimshaw, 1997)

> 'When they do these care plans, they say 'Do you want to say anything?' but they don't listen.'
> Cheryl

Children also usually have very little say at all in placement decisions (Thomas and O'Kane, 1998) and disabled children are particularly unlikely to be consulted in decisions about their care (Morris, 1998b).

> 'No-one asked me whether I wanted to go away to school. It was all talked about behind my back.'
> Mike Owen

Whilst policymakers and practitioners may acknowledge the need to listen to children and young people, the priority accorded to their views is often low. For example, 'the need to listen more closely to the views of young people about the running of children's homes' was last on the list of 15 features which the Warner report identified should be 'kept uppermost in people's minds' (Department of Health, 1992). The Department of Health's report on messages from research included only two pages on 'The young person's perspective' at the end of a 112-page report (Department of Health, 1998a).

We don't know enough about the experience of care from children's points of view

> 'I was at boarding school and I used to come home near enough every weekend to a different family. And eventually I ended up at The Mead. Then I went to a different foster carer and that broke down. I had a feeling that they didn't want me, because all the time I used to go out, do me own thing, come back to the house, there's no-one in when I came back from school, you're coming back, there's no-one in, you don't know what time they'll be back. I felt they didn't want me. I kept going out later. I found it difficult to cope with them.'
>
> David Pearce

> 'When you come into the care system, you need help because that's why you're coming in and you don't get the emotional help you need. They're not encouraging you, they're not assisting you, they're just thinking of the quickest route and the cheapest route. They don't assess you as an individual. They assess you as how much money you're going to cost them because it's all about their budgets.'
>
> Melissa Berry

There is little in the current body of research which concerns the direct experience of children and young people, for example, 'We know almost nothing about how children view foster care, or its impact on them' (Daniel and Ivatts, 1998, p. 211). Research concerning placement outcomes has very rarely included looking at how children themselves understand and cope with their experiences (Jackson and Thomas, 1999). Jackson and Thomas also point out that much research on placement breakdown focuses on the characteristics of the children. This makes it difficult to avoid 'problematising' children who experience placement breakdown, rather than focusing on the problems such an experience creates for them. As Jackson and Thomas say:

'Much instability is created by institutional factors [the way social services departments and other organisations work, local and central government policies], rather than by characteristics of children or their placements. However, these have attracted less attention from researchers.'
(Jackson and Thomas, 1999, p. 41)

The importance of finding out directly from children about their experiences is highlighted by the important issues raised by research which does seek their views. For example, a review of such research (Hill, 1997) points out that, while research and practice has been preoccupied with child–adult relationships:

'Children themselves highlight the importance of child-child relationships. They point to the importance of sustaining contacts among siblings or with friends; recognising and supporting the role and needs of foster carers' own children; having in place explicit policies and processes for dealing with bullying and racism in residential care.'
(Hill, 1997, p. 26)

Schools are sometimes not very good at responding to looked after children's needs

'An example which I think illustrates what is wrong with the attitude within schools to looked after children is the contrast between the pastoral care given to a child who has experienced a bereavement and the attitude to a child removed from his home. The school sees themselves as having a role to support a child whose parent or sibling has died, as being on the side of the child, as being there for the child. They see the problem as being an experience which is awful for the child. And then there is the child who is suddenly separated from their parents, wider family, and maybe neighbourhood. And it might not have been the first time. And they may have been abused. And they've got to go to a new school. And they are having the sort of reactions that I as an adult would have, never mind a child. It manifests itself in school because that's where they go every day. The first barrier that the child experiences is the label 'in care'. If we could describe the problem without alluding to the care system, you'd have a fighting chance of the adults behaving differently. Some of it is well-intentioned resignation – they think the child is beyond help. But some of it is straightforward identifying the child as the problem.'

Barbara Fletcher, Education Policy Officer, Local Government Association

'When I was in school, I was really quite naughty. I would outsmart them in a way that they would count as misbehaving. And the teacher would try and put me down and he knew that if he said things about what was going on with my family and things it would shut me up. It was like a weapon, they knew they couldn't physically hit us, so they would just make us feel as hurt as we made them feel. Just rub it in.'

Danny Carter

Teachers are just as likely as the rest of us to be influenced by the generally negative public attitudes to children in public care. There are also institutional pressures which can get in the way of doing the best for looked after children. The pressure on schools to do well in the league tables of SATs, GCSEs and A levels can also make them wary of children whom it is thought will pull the school's results down. There is evidence that schools are more likely to exclude 'difficult pupils who are already known to be in care' and the education system is now recognised to be failing looked after children (Social Services Inspectorate and Ofsted, 1995).

> 'They weren't all that bothered, so I weren't all that bothered.'
>
> Paula

The attitudes of individual teachers and the general ethos of a school can make a major difference to how looked after children experience education:

'Schools differed considerably in their attitude towards pupils who were looked after: some were welcoming and supportive while others were extremely wary, believing that all looked after children represented a difficulty.'

(Fletcher-Campbell, 1997, p. 138)

All children hate being identified as different in some way. Teachers therefore have to tread a fine line between being supportive and recognising the particular needs that may be associated with coming into care, and identifying and treating the child as different from their peers.

> 'I get treated like I'm different to everybody else. The kids and the teachers, they've been brought up by their mums and dads. They haven't been through the experience. I think they should treat me like any normal person, not as if I'm different to the whole of the school.'
>
> David Pearce

> 'Some teachers don't like you or they're more strict with you than anyone else because you're in care.

'And then some teachers don't really care if you don't do nothing, they say, 'Oh, you've got problems, don't worry.' And that's what annoys you, you just want to be treated like everyone else. You don't want to be treated different.'

Melanie Brooker

'I think they should mind their business. Every time I get in trouble, it's like, 'Oh, your social worker said you're going to be a bit funny today', 'You've just had contact with your Mum', or whatever, and telling me how my life is, instead of asking me. They say things like that in front of 26 children in the class and put you down, and tell people your business. I don't want everyone to know that.'

Danny Carter

Those who work in the care system are not always very good at enabling looked after children to get the most out of the education system

'The under-achievement of looked after children is a tribute to the power of parents. The education system requires parents to do all sorts of things in order that children get the best out of the education system. The current system works well if you have a parent who is pushy and aspiring and a good advocate. The corporate parent is none of these things.'

Barbara Fletcher, Education Policy Officer,
Local Government Association

If children do not have adults in their lives who care about their progress at school, care that they get to school and on time, that they have friends at school, that they aren't bullied, that they do their homework, then there is an additional burden put on their own shoulders in terms of getting the best out of education. Many children in the public care system will not have the resources or the resilience and therefore have a particular need for a 'pushy parent'.

Some foster carers and residential workers do not have the resources or experience themselves to fulfil this role, and there is often no expectation that they will, or support provided to help them do this.

> 'The residential care workers in that unit wouldn't dream of sitting down with a child with a book. They don't do it with their own children.'
>
> Leaving Care Project Worker

Although the different statutory agencies are committed to joint working, it has proved difficult for them to put this into practice

> 'The care system fragments people's lives. As a parent myself, my child's life revolves around her welfare, her education, her health, her social activities, everything is there, it's not fragmented into little bits. But that's what the care system did to me.'
>
> Maggie Lane

Joint working with social services, education and health authorities has been the intention for a number of years now, both at local and national level. Yet there has been a gap between intention and practice. Health, education and social services authorities often have strategies and policies about inter-agency and multidisciplinary working. However, these written documents are not always translated into practice and there is often very little monitoring or evaluation of the extent to which the aims of joint working are being achieved.

One of the key barriers identified by those concerned with improving the education experiences of looked after children was the different values held by social services and education departments.

> 'Education and social services operate within two different legislative agendas and frameworks and culturally they're worlds apart: one is a universal

service and one is targeted on need. These aren't excuses, they are the context in which we have to work.'
>Barbara Fletcher, Education Policy Officer, Local Government Association

'My social worker didn't know how to apply for a grant for me to go to college.'
>John Kohlasch

In the past, the failure of different agencies to work together at local level has also been reflected in the lack of coordination of policy at central government level, although current government initiatives, such as Quality Protects and the Social Exclusion Unit, are attempting to address this.

'If you're working with children and families, then the benefits system and how it operates affects what you can achieve, because poverty is such a big issue. Hitherto, I have never known real across-the-board coordination of policy in relation to children at central government level.'
>Sir William Utting

Policy and practice are not sufficiently informed by research

'There is not a culture of considering how best research findings can be introduced into practice. For example, the two research studies by York University [Whittaker, Archer and Hicks, 1997; Sinclair and Gibbs, 1998] brought forward a wealth of evidence about what makes children's homes work, in terms of what is it about staff teams, the character of the establishment, which seem to make for good outcomes for young people. And yet, I don't think these findings are infiltrating practice enough.'
>Steve Hart, Social Services Inspector, London West Inspection Group

What gets in the way of change? 25

Policy and practice is influenced by stronger, and more unpredictable, factors than just research findings. For example, some people have argued that the changing political context in the late 1990s has meant that previous messages about working in partnership with parents – which meant fewer children on child protection registers and being brought into the public care system – have now been replaced by a more interventionist message, and a concurrent rise in the number of looked after children. Policies and practices are changing at local level, but with very little reference to what research tells us about how children are best protected and their welfare promoted.

> 'The fashions of practice and policy swing so quickly sometimes that by the time research comes out – which might have been commissioned five years ago – the context has changed so dramatically that the findings no longer seem relevant. It can sometimes be difficult applying the lessons of research, even if people are minded to do so, because the context has changed.'
> Ray Jones, Director of Social Services, Wiltshire County Council

David Berridge pointed out that, although his research review on foster care identified some 170 studies which commented on foster care services, he could only identify 13 major research studies with foster care as their central focus. As he says, this is 'inconsistent with the major role currently fulfilled by foster care for children looked after by local authorities' (Berridge, 1997, p. 9).

> 'We take action to tackle the problem as we see it. How we see the problem depends on our knowledge of it, which is always partial, and the current thinking about children, their parents and the role of the local authority.'
> Sir William Utting

Research findings are often used to fit the current fashion

> 'I worry that we read research too selectively. We go for the big messages and forget the riders underneath. I also don't think our critical appraisal skills are as good as they should be. To be honest, some pretty grand conclusions are drawn from some pretty ropey research sometimes. It's not about evidence, it's about something to hang bias on.'
>
> Ray Jones, Director of Social Services, Wiltshire County Council

When research is used to inform policy and practice, there is sometimes a tendency to use it selectively, to back up the current political fashion or professional 'wisdom'. What kind of research is commissioned, how it is done and how it is used are all influenced by the political and social context of the time.

> 'Research about disabled children's experiences has been selectively used to justify cuts in services – on the grounds that residential care was universally a bad idea, although I did try to say that's not quite what the research says.'
>
> Service Manager (Disabled Children), Social Services Department, County Council

We are entering a period when there will be more pressure on local authorities to place children for adoption. There is more research on adoption than on any other form of placement, and more is in the pipeline (together with a review of research commissioned by the Department of Health). The evidence suggests that adoption offers the best chance of stability for many looked after children: the message from central government is that local authorities are not doing enough to make adoption possible for such children. Nevertheless, many social workers are nervous that this is yet another political fashion, and that the resulting pressure to arrange adoptions will mean that some decisions are made which are not, in fact, in the interests of individual children.

One of the people who read a draft of this report commented on the generosity of the young people interviewed. While astute in their criticisms of the system which has so blatantly failed them, still they were understanding of the constraints within which individual workers often try to do their best for the young people in their care.

The point is, however, that as a society we cannot be excused the way we have failed these children and young people. We have to ask ourselves what is needed to change the all too common situation where young people are leaving the care system more damaged than when they entered it. This was the second question posed to those interviewed and their responses help to structure the second part of this report.

2 What helps to bring about change for the better?

This section of the report concerns the points that respondents made when asked the question 'What helps or would help to bring about change for the better?' Some people identified initiatives and developments which they felt were already changing things for the better and some focused more on what still needs to be done.

Changing public attitudes towards looked after children

'We should do something with the public, so the public can get to know us, so that we are part of the community. So that it proves to them that kids in children's homes aren't as bad as they think they are.'

Derek Sewell

'The kids' home is in such a little village. When I first went there two years ago, they all hated us, we were the problem kids, it's our fault we're in care sort of thing. Over the years, it's changed. I wrote a letter for the local parish newspaper saying how unfair it is we're treated differently, we've done nothing wrong, the majority of kids in care have been abused, it's not because they're naughty and all that. Eventually, slowly, it's getting the point across in the village. They're being politer, we're getting more contact with them and all that. When I first went there it was so isolated, we were like over here and they were over there and they didn't want to know us.'

Melanie Brooker

All the groups of young people spoken to for this report identified that public attitudes towards looked after children had to be changed. They had ideas themselves about how this could be done, which included strategies for challenging local preconceptions about children's homes and foster care, as well as ideas for national publicity about looked after children.

One common message was that any attempt to challenge public attitudes towards looked after children had to involve children and young people themselves. 'Nothing about us without us' is a phrase which sums up their message and they were particularly critical of campaigns by child care organisations which had not consulted children in care.

The young people also talked about how important it was to influence the attitudes of the general public, because social workers and all those who work with children are drawn from the ranks of the general public. They felt it was particularly important to challenge teachers' attitudes towards looked after children, something which social services departments also stressed.

> 'They should make an advert on TV saying it's nothing big to be in a foster home. Because then people get a better understanding about it. It's like they hear 'There's an alien just landed near London Bridge' – but if you make it known that there's aliens all over the gaff, no-one's going to think it's strange, are they?'
>
> Danny Carter

> 'We should remember that social workers, managers of children's homes, whatever, were once Joe Public and really we need to re-educate the public, so that everybody who comes into social work in the future has an awareness that children and young people aren't mad and bad and sad and all the other rubbish we get labelled with.'
>
> Maggie Lane

In our attempts to change public attitudes towards looked after children, it is important to emphasise that, in taking children and young people into public care, local authorities are fulfilling a duty – on behalf of us all – to promote and protect their human rights. Article 20 of the UN Convention on the Rights of the Child states that children whose family cannot look after them are 'entitled to special protection and assistance provided by the State'. As UNICEF points out, the use of the word 'entitled' is significant.

> 'It goes to the heart of the duty all societies owe children – that if parents cannot meet children's needs, then children have a moral claim on the rest of us.'
> UNICEF, 1998, p. 259

Attitudes towards looked after children will also be affected by attitudes towards children in general. Greater recognition of children's human rights would help. Here, the government, the media and other institutions have a role to play – and must take responsibility for the continuing contravention of children's human rights.

> 'There is still scope for government and national institutions to try to move public opinion along in a more liberal direction as far as children are concerned and produce a greater consensus about the way they should be regarded.'
> Sir William Utting

Listening to and involving children and young people

The 1989 Children Act and accompanying guidance make many references to children's entitlements to be consulted and involved in decisions about their care. As a result, there are an increasing number of resources which aim to help involve children in assessments, reviews and care plans. These include the National Children's Bureau's *It's Your Meeting: A guide to help young people get the most from their reviews* (Wheal and Sinclair, 1995) and The Children's Society's *I'll Go First: The Planning and Review Toolkit for use with children with disabilities* (The Children's Society, 1997).

> 'One young man whom I saw said that his voice had been heard in a review and a plan had been made in a way which conveyed to him that he was an important person, that he had some power.'
>
> Steve Hart, Social Services Inspector,
> London West Inspection Group

Much more attention is now being paid to the need to consult with and involve looked after children and young people at all levels, from individual assessments to the planning of services. Under the Quality Protects initiative, £5 million is being spent in 1999/2000 from the special social services grant in promoting opportunities for 'listening to children'. There are also opportunities under the Best Value initiative, as consultation with service users is a key requirement. The London Borough of Newham, for example, carried out a consultation exercise with looked after children which involved a postal questionnaire and telephone interviews, and visits to children with communication and/or cognitive impairments (London Borough of Newham 1999a, 1999b). Children's Rights Officers and Advocates (CROA) are developing a training pack to equip local authority social services staff and elected members to involve looked after children and young people in decision-making about their own lives.

There is increasing recognition that children with communication impairments also have an entitlement to be consulted and involved. Some people are developing good practice in this area, for example the consultation with children with learning difficulties who use a residential service in East Sussex (Triangle, 1999a). Such initiatives mean changing our methods of communication to suit the children involved, as the authors explain:

'A range of approaches were used and the young people communicated their views through speech, sign, symbols, body language, facial expression, gesture, behaviour, art, photographs, objects of reference, games, drawing and playing.'

(Triangle, 1999b, p. 5)

If children and young people are genuinely involved, not just in the decisions about their own individual situations, but also in the development of policies and practice concerning looked after children, this in itself will change organisational cultures. As Linda Marshall, Children's Rights Adviser, Essex County Council, says, 'It's the way people work with children which empowers them.'

It is also important to value the strength that children get from coming together with those who have similar experiences:

> 'I think we've succeeded in making people listen to us. If we're all in a group together, then we're stronger.'
>
> Katrina Doe

> 'This [group] is better for us than any social worker, any counsellor, or anything like that, because we're talking to people who been there, and we can have a laugh. It's an emotional support at a base level. It does more and it costs less than any social worker.'
>
> John Kohlasch

Developing a culture within local authorities and child care organisations which is based on recognising children's human rights

> 'I think children who are coming into the care system have a right to expect that resources will be configured in a way which meets children's needs.'
>
> Steve Hart, Social Services Inspector, London West Inspection Group

A rights-based perspective needs to run through everything that is done by all those involved with looked after children. Some social services departments have adopted the UN Convention on the Rights of the Child and there is scope for looking in detail at how these rights can be implemented for looked after children.

'We're suggesting that the UN Convention on the Rights of the Child, as an underpinning framework, would provide us with some common principles and standards to work for in relation to all children and young people. Because it's universal, non-party political, it's a way of moving forward with all our partners, in education, etc, having some common base to start off from.'

Linda Marshall, Children's Rights Adviser,
Essex County Council

Human rights are about recognising our common humanity, about aspiring for all human beings what we would want for ourselves.

'It is very important the councillors and senior managers understand the nature of their parental responsibilities [for looked after children]. They should always ask themselves whether the arrangements they make for this child are the ones they would want for their own child. If you apply this, then you will be doing the best you can with the resources you've got.'

Sir William Utting

A value base which has human rights at its centre would also recognise that these human rights apply to all children. Article 2 of the UN Convention states that the rights apply to all children 'without discrimination of any kind' and that

'States Parties shall take all appropriate measures to ensure that the child is protected against all forms of discrimination.'

Sometimes, however, children's status and experience of being in public care gets in the way of their rights to education, to be heard, to privacy, to be free from harm, to health services, and so on. In addition, services for children sometimes fail to respond appropriately to other aspects of a child's experience and needs and this results in their human rights being contravened. If we start from the position that all children have the same human rights, this would help, for example, to recognise that children with communication impairments have a right to be consulted, that children who need tube feeding have a right to education, that children with autism have the right to a family life, that children from a minority ethnic background have the right to a cultural identity.

Harnessing local democratic structures to address the needs of looked after children

'It was very helpful that the Secretary of State wrote to all local authority councillors reminding them of their parental responsibilities and that looking after children properly required all the resources of the authority and this wasn't a job just to be sidelined to social services departments. If you're going to look after young people properly, you do need the housing, leisure and all aspects of the local authority working with you.'

Sir William Utting

'In Ealing they set up a Members' Task Group to monitor the progress of the Action Plan following the inspection report. That group lives on, it still meets on a monthly basis to look at children's issues. The group has always been cross-party and has become extremely successful. It now includes senior managers from housing, education, health, two young people, one from foster care, one from residential, the community paediatric consultant, the consultant for child and adolescent mental health. It's a well-supported, healthy working group, chaired by the Chair of Social Services but with representation from all the political parties. They've put aside their differences to work actively to achieve a working group which simply devotes its time to children's issues and nothing else.'

John Skinner, Assistant Director (Children and Families), London Borough of Ealing

People have identified that it was helpful that, at the start of the Quality Protects initiative, the Secretary of State for Health wrote to all councillors reminding them of their responsibilities as corporate parents. The general message that 'we should want for these children what we want for our own children' is one that needs to hit home, particularly in areas where political conflict has sometimes got in the way of the local politicians working together to deliver good quality services.

In November 1999, the Department of Health and the Local Government Association jointly launched 'Think Child! The Councillor's Guide to Quality Protects'. This publication set out councillors' role in the Quality Protects initiative, included examples of good practice and questions which councillors needed to address in order to play their full part (Department of Health and Local Government Association, 1999).

The message is also that being a good parent is not just the responsibility of social services departments, but concerns all functions of the local authority. Moreover, it is important that local decision-making structures open themselves up to be influenced by young people themselves. This is not only about inviting young people as representatives of looked after children onto committees and working groups, but also about developing communication, consultation and decision-making processes which are best suited to children and young people.

> 'Consulting with and involving children is not an add-on, it has to frame how you go about doing the work. The whole organisation has to take responsibility for listening to children and not hive it off to particular postholders. I have to keep sending back requests saying, 'I'm sorry, I'm not a purveyor of young people's views'. You have to look at how you interact with young people who are using services, how are you going to build this involvement, this consultation into what you do.'
> Linda Marshall, Children's Rights Adviser,
> Essex County Council

Monitoring what goes on and applying sanctions when the care that is provided is not good enough

Many of the current government's initiatives concern monitoring and inspection of how local authorities are doing. The National Care Standards Commission, to be set up in 2002, may also mean that more attention will be given to the performance of the private and voluntary sector, as well as local authority services. Inspections by the Social Services Inspectorate and their Joint Reviews with the Audit Commission pick up whether and how social services departments are fulfilling their statutory duties. The Department of Health has significant sanctions at its disposal, including powers under the Local Government Act 1999 to intervene when local authorities fail to meet standards laid down under the Best Value framework.

When, in recent years, inspections of some social services departments revealed that large numbers of looked after children did not have an allocated social worker, the authorities concerned were left in no doubt of the high stakes involved if improvements were not made. These authorities were also criticised for not having enough family-based placements and for the over-use of residential placements outside their areas. It would also be possible for inspections and the Department of Health generally to be equally strong in their messages and actions concerning other aspects of social services departments' statutory duties, in particular, the requirements to 'ascertain the wishes and feelings' of children, and to target services to meet individual needs.

> 'If I was a child, the kind of questions which would indicate whether things were changing for the better would be: Was I being listened to? Did people really understand what had happened to me and my family? Did I have a future? Did I know what was going to happen in the future and did I have a say in the decisions about my future? You have to sit down and talk to children in order to find out whether these are their experiences.'
>
> Steve Hart, Social Services Inspector,
> London West Inspection Group

As we have seen, there are clear messages coming from the current government about targets, outcomes and generally what local authorities are expected to deliver. Many of these initiatives have a direct impact on looked after children. The Performance Assessment Framework, part of the Best Value initiative, has made possible the first national picture of the quality of social services. The first analysis of how social services departments are doing on a number of different indicators revealed, for example, that some did particularly badly in key areas such as inspecting children's homes and providing long-term foster placements (Department of Health, 1999c).

However, it is unclear yet how much information about local authorities' performance in terms of the Quality Protects targets will be published. Those who use services, those who vote for local politicians and those who pay taxes have a right to know how local authorities are doing. Although the Social Services Inspectorate and the Audit Commission publish their Joint Reviews, these are expensive and not very accessible to members of the public. While some may say that 'league tables' based on Quality Protects and other targets don't give the whole picture, the information should be in the public domain and the subject of debate. In the past, the emphasis has often been on the failings of young people in the care system. In the future, we need to focus more on the failings, and successes, of the social organisations which look after them.

Resource implications of doing the best for looked after children

> 'The government has to recognise the resource implications of what it wants local authorities to do. Something like 80–85 per cent of social services money comes by way of government grant.'
> Sir William Utting

All parents know that the more money you have, the easier it is to do the best for your children. Two of the clearest messages from children and young people are:

- They often feel pushed into unsuitable placements because that is all that is available.
- They want more access to independent advocates (Voice for the Child in Care, 1998).

Both of these issues have obvious resource implications, which were recognised by the House of Commons Select Committee on Health when it recommended, for example, that those placing looked after children should have access to a range of residential and fostering placements (House of Commons Select Committee on Health, 1998, para 172).

Things are improving in terms of resources: social services directors have welcomed an increase in resources announced by the Government in November 1999 and the three-year special grant for Quality Protects is particularly important. Nevertheless, services for looked after children have been starved of adequate resources for many years. In the same week that the increased government funding for social services was announced, Birmingham City Council said it was considering selling off some of its children's homes because it does not have sufficient resources to pay for necessary repairs and maintenance ('Community Care', 2–8 December 1999, p. 4).

Of course, it is what you do with the money which is important – but this shouldn't obscure the fact that more resources are needed. For example, it is recognised good practice that, in the context of each foster placement, the foster carer needs a support worker, the child needs a social worker, and therefore each placement needs to be supported by two workers.

> 'The child gets a visit from their social worker every week. They need someone to do direct work with them, not just someone to take them on a contact visit but who is qualified and experienced to support them and nurture the placement. The foster carer also has a support worker.'
> Jane Westacott, Barnardo's, Colchester

In many cases, a lot of intensive support is required to enable a placement to work. However, social services departments often do not have the resources to do this.

It also needs to be recognised that residential care workers, if they are to build up supportive relationships with young people, need support themselves. Current management and resourcing of residential homes may not be sufficient to provide this support and this may not be solely about the more efficient use of resources, but about having more resources in the first place.

> 'I really felt on my own. I had no support from my manager: she was supposed to give me supervision but she often cancelled because something else had come up, she was under a lot of pressure herself. I think we should have ongoing training on working with the very difficult young people that we have to deal with. And I need someone to advise me what to do, to tell me whether what I'm doing is OK. You know, you want to do your best for them but sometimes you just want to hide in the office, it's very difficult to know what to do.'
>
> Residential care worker in a town in the north-east of England

The Safeguards Review recognised that some inadequacies of the care system resulted from 'what might collectively and charitably be described as inefficiency' (Utting, 1997, p. 198). However, the Review also concluded that:

'it is impressed by the consistency with which representative and other bodies have communicated the difficulty of resourcing their services [and] accepts that some of the shortcomings it has learned about arise from the scarcity of money and other resources such as skilled and experienced staff.'

(Utting, 1997, p. 198)

A national strategy for residential care

> 'Something needs to be done about the image of residential care, upping the status of residential work, giving it a clear function. Certainly people in residential work feel undervalued and at the butt end of the service.'
>
> Steve Hart, Social Services Inspector, London West Inspection Group

> 'I know we should work with neighbouring authorities and the independent sector to plan services – but the reality is that we don't. It needs a much bigger intervention than we're ever going to do on our own, if we're to have the residential provision we need to make good placements.'
>
> Senior manager, social services department in the north-east of England

The Government's review of safeguards for children living away from home recommended that the Department of Health should develop a national strategy for residential child care, emphasising that:

'Urgent action is needed to raise standards, but the sector now lacks enough providers of sufficient size to organise and achieve this from within. Government action is needed to implement a strategy to drive up standards all round.'

(Utting, 1997, p. 2)

The Warner Report (Department of Health, 1992) on the recruitment, management and training of staff in children's homes was followed by the establishment of the Support Force for Children's Residential Care which developed a Code of Practice for employing residential workers (Support Force for Children's Residential Care, 1995). The Children's Services Plans which also followed the Warner Report were intended to 'identify needs and the means of meeting these' (Department of Health, 1992, p. 174), but the recent national inspection of children's services planning concluded that:

'Children's Services Plans are not yet established as inter-agency documents that lead to the development of services for children in need in most local authorities.'
(Social Services Inspectorate, 1999d, p. 1)

The need for a national strategy for residential care remains. The Association of Metropolitan Authorities told the House of Commons Select Committee on Health:

'I do not think we know what the appropriate level of residential care should be within a particular locality for a particular child population.'
(House of Commons Select Committee on Health, 1998, para. 166)

The Select Committee concluded:

'There is a clear need for an increase in the number of children's homes countrywide, to enable local authorities to make appropriate placements, to reduce problems arising within homes from an inappropriate 'mix' of children, and to relieve pressure on the fostering service' (para. 170).

Any national or local strategies on residential care must consult with children and young people. Those who use the service have ideas about what kind of services work best for them. One research study, which included interviews with 223 young people in children's homes, concluded that social services departments should aim to:

- keep their homes as small as possible;
- appoint heads of homes who have a clear philosophy, are agreed with the management on the way the home should be run, are sensitive to the deeply-felt concerns of residents, and are capable of uniting the staff group behind them;
- encourage contact with families, but remain sensitive to the wish of many residents to stay in contact with their families but not to live with them.
(Sinclair and Gibbs, 1998, summarised in Department of Health, 1998a)

> 'In Bolton they have small units, like normal houses, with only two or three young people. And there's a staff team of three who actually live in the place when they're on duty. And that's so much better than places with lots of children and lots of staff.'
>
> Maggie Lane

Increase the number of foster carers, pay them, and train and support them in the work they do

If social services departments have an adequate pool of foster carers from which to choose when placing a child, then placement decisions are more likely to be needs-led rather than service-led and placement breakdown therefore would be less common. Research has found the following factors help to create this situation:

- a clear strategy for foster care;
- specialist family placement teams;
- targeted recruitment campaigns for foster carers;
- payment which recognises the levels of expertise and care required;
- ongoing support to foster carers from social workers;
- ongoing training for foster carers.

Research also tells us that 'quality services do not come cheap' (Berridge, 1997, p. 79). Some organisations are moving away from the voluntary nature of foster care, recognising that this is skilled work which needs training, ongoing support and should be accorded proper pay and status.

> 'We try and work on an equal basis with our Bridge foster carers [who provide short-term emergency placements]. We try to give them the same conditions of service and the same feeling of being valued that we aim to give our social workers. We give them supervision which is properly recorded. We've developed a career grade, so there's a senior Bridge carer grade that they can move onto ... If you're expecting people to work on an equal level, then you've got an equal right to say there are

aspects of the way you're doing this job which need to improve. That comes with the pay, the perks, the same way that our social workers are tackled. And that creates a dialogue because, equally, they will tackle us if they aren't happy with the way we are doing our job.'
>Jane Westacott, Barnardo's, Colchester

Giving foster carers proper payment for the work that they are doing, recognising the support that they need to do the job (which sometimes includes respite from caring for a child), does not necessarily mean moving away from offering a child a caring, nurturing relationship. Rather, it is about recognising what is necessary in order to create and sustain such a relationship.

'When I first introduced respite for Bridge foster carers, there was resistance – from the foster carers, and from the social workers. There was a feeling that families were supposed to take these children on and love them and care for them all the time. But actually, if you build in respite, you don't get the downward spiral of people getting negative and tired and punitive towards the child. It helps keep them above that line, it helps keep them positive. So that they can do a more professional job of caring for the child. The professionalism of the foster carer has not resulted in them doing a more distant job. It has resulted in them being able to get closer to the child and sustain the closeness.'
>Jane Westacott, Barnardo's, Colchester

There is also evidence that, if foster carers are to be recruited who will meet the needs of children from all parts of the community, specific attention has to be paid to this. In particular, there appears to be:

'a direct relationship between availability of carers from minority ethnic groups and the recruitment of family placement workers whose culture and ethnicity reflected those of the children requiring placement.'
>(Waterhouse, 1997)

'Word of mouth is the best form of recruitment you could ever have. I've been a foster carer for 17 years. They know that and they know me. So they'll listen to me. I know the community. They need to get the message that the organisation appreciates them and needs them.'

Norma Kelman, Foster Carer Coordinator

Any foster care strategy, at local or national level, must address the particular barriers to providing good foster care for particular groups of children, in particular for disabled children and black and minority ethnic children.

Paying attention to the way organisations treat their staff

Social services departments need a vision of what they want to achieve for the children they look after. Such a vision is no good, however, if it is merely written down on paper, or only held by those at the top of the organisation.

'Proof of the commitment of the people at the top is absolutely crucial. Written procedures are useless, if they just stay as written procedures. Councillors, directors, senior managers must convey this to social workers, must say to them, 'I am here to tell you this, to share this with you, to discuss with you the problems you encounter'. None of this is going to come off the printed page.'

Sir William Utting

'I described in the first inspection in Ealing a 'culture of hopelessness'. That certainly wasn't there in the second inspection. They had a very clear vision of where they were going, they had some clear tasks to achieve ... They were very keen to have staff appraisal and organisational development very closely linked to individual staff development.'

Steve Hart, Social Services Inspector,
London West Inspection Group

What helps to bring about change for the better? 45

'A lot of the early work was trying to engage staff and include them in the new agenda, and to convince them that they were going to have an active part to play in developing the new culture and structure. That's very difficult unless you really mean it and unless there's some visible evidence for staff that you really do operate in that particular way.'

John Skinner, Assistant Director (Children and Families), London Borough of Ealing

Social workers and residential care workers consulted for the purpose of this report talked about what helped them to do their jobs properly. This included:

- being valued for their strengths;
- being supported in areas of their work that they found difficult;
- good, regular supervision that is recorded and action taken when required;
- realistic caseloads;
- high quality ongoing training and other resources, such as access to a library and contact with good practice initiatives by other agencies.

'Everybody can go to [the training], social workers, foster carers, adoptive parents. We have real front-line stuff which makes us feel things are possible. It's inspiring really.'

Jan Kavanagh, Barnardo's, Colchester

Social workers and residential care workers also talked about the importance of having senior managers who were approachable, open with front-line staff about what was going on, and who liked meeting and working with children.

The Social Services Inspectorate has found that the key to changing the performance of a social services department is 'the quality and competence of front-line managers' (Social Services Inspectorate, 1999c, p. 3). Front-line managers have the key role of:

- determining whether standards of practice are consistently maintained;
- supporting staff engaged in complex, personally demanding practice;
- ensuring staff are continually developed in knowledge-based practice.

(Social Services Inspectorate, 1999c, p. 3)

The Social Services Inspectorate intends to focus on the quality of front-line management in future inspections. The ability of organisations to recruit, develop and support good front-line managers is undoubtedly a test of how effectively they nurture and maximise the abilities and performance of staff at all levels.

Skills, training and attitudes required by social workers and care workers

As Renuka Jeyarajah Dent, Deputy Chief Executive at The Bridge Child Care Development Service, says, 'As a child, you need someone to tell you that you're beautiful and special' ('Community Care', 13–19 May 1999, p. 19). People should only be employed as social workers, residential care workers, or recruited as foster carers if they genuinely like children. This may seem a trite thing to say, but the fact is that there are people employed within the child care system who quite obviously do *not* like children and this clearly has devastating consequences for the children they care for.

> 'People who go on social work courses should be people who care about children.'
>
> Rachel Smith

> 'The most important thing to look for when recruiting social workers is whether they like children.'
>
> Steve Hart, Social Services Inspector, London West Inspection Group

> 'I'm less concerned about people's academic abilities and more concerned about how they

relate to people. I'd like to see us valuing people's life experiences more, and what those experiences enable them to bring to social work.'
> John Skinner, Assistant Director (Children and Families), London Borough of Ealing

The assessment of attitudes and inter-personal skills, therefore, has to be a key part of recruitment and appraisal of staff. Research on children's homes has identified the kinds of skills required, if residential workers are to work successfully with children:

'Necessary skills included a range of listening, observing, intervening and assessment competencies, in order to understand emotional reactions and feelings in the young people and in themselves, and to work effectively across the whole range of tasks.'
> (Department of Health 1998a, p. 82, referring to Whittaker, Archer and Hicks, 1997)

The research identified not only the personal qualities required for good care but also the qualities which indicate that someone is not suitable for such work. Young people would say that organisations generally need to be much more stringent about the kind of people they employ to look after children.

> 'Social workers should take an emotional course, so that they understand how kids are destroyed emotionally. They shouldn't learn it from a book but by talking to kids.'
>
> Cheryl

> 'I feel that my current line manager values the skills I bring from having been a parent myself, and that I'm expected to put a lot of myself into the relationship with the kids here. You feel those abilities are recognised by the organisation and that's how you get on, that's how you progress in your career, by helping these kids to work things out.'
>
> Residential care worker

The importance of the relationship between social worker and child

One of the most striking things that came out of talking to the 35 young people was their high expectations of social workers. As we have seen, they were very critical of social workers' failure to spend enough time with them or listen to them enough, yet understanding of the difficulties that social workers have doing their job, and full of praise for those who did it well.

> 'He took me out places, he did things with me, he did things that got my spirits up that made me feel what's the point of just sitting about mucking around. He kept me on a straight line, he was strict. He was always firm about what I did. If he heard that I'd been naughty at school, he'd be like a father, he'd come and say 'That is not on'. He would never be angry, he'd just be strict, firm in his voice, the way he spoke to me. He would tell me stuff about what would happen if I carried on doing those things.'
>
> Sean Linney

> 'It never felt like she wanted to go. Some social workers are like, 'Oh, I'll see you then', and then they only want ten minutes and then they go. She had a limited time allowance, but she didn't make it so she couldn't be bothered and just needed to go. She'd make you feel like she wanted to be there, she wanted to listen.'
>
> Melanie Brooker

> 'He talked to me like I was a person, not just another piece of his pay cheque.'
>
> John Kohlasch

For many children in public care their social worker is the embodiment of their looked after status and almost all the young people consulted for the purpose of this report expressed the opinion (entirely unprompted) that social workers should spend more time with them and take a greater interest in their progress. While foster carers or residential care workers could play an important role in their lives, they still had high expectations of social workers and at times spoke in terms of social workers having the responsibilities of a parent (which of course they do, as representatives of the local authority who has taken parental responsibility).

> 'It's just like with a family, you don't have just one person to look after you. You need a social worker to care, even if you've got a good relationship with your foster carer. I reckon you should have someone who you can just go to.'
>
> Laura Stephens

We know that close attachments to one or two significant adults (not necessarily parents) make a major difference to the way children experience situations which are potentially emotionally damaging. Young people have identified that they expect social workers to be significant parts of their lives, not to be merely passing through, filling in forms, chairing reviews, arranging contact visits. This view concurs with that expressed by Mike Leadbetter, Director of Social Services in Essex, when he said:

'I believe it's essential that we engage on a really deep level with children, in ways that hurt sometimes ... Social workers need to reassert their professional place, working up close with children.'

('Community Care', 13–19 May 1999, p. 19)

The House of Commons Select Committee on Health concluded that looked after children would be better served if

'better-trained and better-resourced social workers were to rediscover their traditional role as confidants and champions of the interests of the children they look after.'

(House of Commons Select Committee on Health, 1998, p. lxxvii)

This is also what many children and young people want. Senior social services managers need to break down the organisational barriers which currently exist and make such a relationship possible.

Adapting services to meet children's and young people's needs

> 'People who live in care aren't any different from anyone else. They should think about what your needs are without labelling you.'
>
> Anthony Hillern

One of the key barriers identified by those consulted for this report was the way in which children and young people in care were expected to fit into services, rather than services being tailored to suit individual children and young people. There are a few examples of services being more flexible and knowledge of how this can be done needs to be better disseminated and social services departments and voluntary organisations encouraged to change the way services are currently organised. Two examples are:

- Barnardo's Family Placement Services in Edinburgh which brought together two previously separate services: time-limited, task-centred foster care; and a permanent family placement service. 'The aim in developing an integrated service was to offer maximum possible continuity and stability for children by providing a full continuum of services from respite care to adoption without the need to transfer children from one placement to another for administrative reasons.' (Jackson and Thomas, 1999, p. 91)
- Jackson and Thomas also highlighted two organisations, the Pro-Teen and the Children's Family Trust, whose commitment to achieving long-term stability for children continues into adulthood. This is in stark contrast to the relationship which most services have with looked after children which is usually determined by administrative and legislative criteria rather than the need that everyone has for a continuing relationship with a caring adult.

> 'I really wanted to carry on seeing Dan [residential care worker] after I left and I didn't see why I couldn't go back sometimes and stay.'
>
> Mick Crosby

> 'The culture of children's services needs to be one that enables flexible provision. Resources are very often hidebound in organisational structures which are often vertical with a sort of silo mentality. There's still the residential arm of the department, there's still the fieldwork arm, there's still day services, and there's someone who liaises with health and education. But the crucial issue is where they integrate horizontally, where do they come together to respond to an individual child and family's need? You need to break it all down, so that they can come together in a package in response to individual need.'
>
> Steve Hart, Social Services Inspector,
> London West Inspection Group

If services are to be needs-led rather than service-led, the way they are funded, organised and what they actually do will often need to be fundamentally re-examined. A key feature of the few services which Jackson and Thomas identified as successfully promoting stable placements was that:

'all allow first-hand carers or workers in regular contact with young people considerable autonomy to use resources in the way that seems most important to them. This in turn allows them to act quickly and decisively to meet needs or defuse crises.'

(Jackson and Thomas, 1999, p. 93)

> 'It was really good because, when I got to the stage where I really wanted to go and talk to someone about the abuse when I was younger, she could pick up the phone and find me someone. It wasn't a case of 'Oh, I'll have to refer you to X and you'll have to have a letter from Y and then wait six months for an appointment'.'
>
> Mira

Services which are needs-led are services which adapt to meet the needs of a particular child. In order to bring this about, however, action is required at a strategic level to develop flexible services. The children's services planning framework could play a more effective role in this than it has up to now.

Meeting all aspects of individual children's needs

The Looked After Children (LAC) documentation will help to ensure that there is attention paid to all aspects of the needs of individual children. Such documentation is only necessary, however, because many looked after children have not had one adult who has taken responsibility for ensuring that they get access to the health care they are entitled to, who has taken an interest in their education, etc. This is an indictment of the extent to which the care system does 'look after' children and the existence of the LAC forms should not obscure children's need for someone to take on this role in their lives.

> 'It's about all the services in your local authority coming together and that means health, education and social services because they all play a part in your life. Just making sure you go to the dentist, for example – who makes sure that happens for someone in care? Because you're moving around so much, so who knows if you've had your check-up, who knows if you had your TB jab?'
>
> Melissa Berry

If health, social services and education authorities are to work together to meet the needs of looked after children, there is a need to move away from the kind of attitude which is about delineating responsibility, an attitude which encourages individual workers to attempt to pass responsibility onto someone else, rather than work together with other professionals.

> 'A health authority representative said that the change in the way social services [in the London Borough of Ealing] are working is extraordinary. I was told 'People are now interested in these children, rather than just trying to get us to see somebody because they didn't have anybody else

to deal with them. It's about what can we all do for this child'.'

Steve Hart, Social Services Inspector,
London West Inspection Group

The Quality Protects framework attempts to promote attention to the health and education needs of looked after children. It is also important to address the needs and aspects of identity which are related to impairments, ethnicity and sexuality. It can make a big difference to children when an important part of their identity is recognised in a positive way.

'We had a new manager took over about a year ago and she actually took the time to sit down with me and say, 'Kavita, what's Diwali all about?' And one day when I came back from school, the whole place was lit up with candles. It was lovely, and they even got me a sari. It was lovely, it made me feel wanted.'

Kavita

Ensuring looked after children get the most out of the education system

'Deciding to do a lot about education is probably the most worthwhile investment social services can make for looked after children. It is something which is going to last and go with that young person. If the local authority can support its foster carers and residential workers, and work with its schools, it can do its best for the children it's responsible for.'

Barbara Fletcher, Education Policy Officer,
Local Government Association

'The children's home I was in was actually very good. They encouraged education. They got me to go to school. The Education Support Teacher hassled me about revising for my exams.'

John Kohlasch

> 'My teacher has made a big difference in my life.'
> Melissa Berry

It is now recognised that the education and care systems have failed most looked after children in terms of their educational achievements. There needs to be a continual challenge to the assumption that some children are just too difficult, and that coming into public care inevitably means that their education will suffer. Research indicates that even the most damaged young people can have positive experiences of education:

> 'There was evidence of remarkable success with some extremely difficult young people where schools were prepared to support and encourage them and work in collaboration with other agencies.'
> (Fletcher-Campbell, 1997, p. 138)

Instead of focusing on looked after children as the problem in terms of their performance at school, we need to focus more on what gets in the way of them getting the most out of their education. For example, if foster carers or residential workers are not comfortable with helping children with their homework, they need training and support to help them fulfil this role.

> 'Officers appointing or selecting carers should ensure either that carers are committed to promoting education for young people for whom they are caring, and able to take the necessary practical measures; or that they are prepared to undergo some sort of formal or informal training in order to assist them to do this. The training could be 'on-the-job' training by education support service workers.'
> (Fletcher-Campbell, 1997, p. 155).)

Three initiatives should help to improve the educational chances for looked after children. Firstly, the Quality Protects initiative includes a sub-objective:

To bring the overall performance of children looked after, for a year or more, at Key Stage SATs and GCSE closer into line with local children generally.

This is backed by a National Priorities Guidance target which, although it has been criticised for being too low, is having an important impact on education departments in that they are now having to pay more attention to the performance of looked after children.

> 'The values of the Education Department are about high achievement and it's only now that they've been given targets for looked after children that we've got a chance of deploying resources into them.'
>
> Alison Williams, Reviewing Officer, Royal Borough of Kensington and Chelsea

The second initiative concerns the guidance issued by the Department for Education and Employment on the education of looked after children, which recommends:

- Every school should have a designated teacher to liaise with social services concerning looked after children.
- Every looked after child should have a Personal Education Plan, covering long-term and short-term goals.
- Placements should only be made where education provision is also secured.
- Local authorities must secure an education placement within 30 days.

Finally, the Looked After Children system of recording information about children should help to keep a track of children's educational achievements and flag up causes for concern.

Tackling bullying in schools

Children and young people spend large amounts of time at school. School can be a very important source of continuity, friendships and feeling good about yourself. Or it can be a daily torture of isolation and bullying. Negative experiences like this will inevitably mean that children lose out in terms of education. It is very important, therefore, that all schools have clear anti-bullying policies, which cover looked after children, and which are rigorously implemented.

'I know it's said a lot but it's true, everyone hates difference. A lot of people hate difference and in a school it's a very small minority who are in care. So we're different from the majority.'

Kurtis Hall

Schools have to tread a fine line between respecting looked after children's right to privacy and encouraging acceptance of them amongst other children. The best place to start when considering how to implement an anti-bullying policy is by consulting children and young people themselves. Those spoken to for the purposes of this report stressed the importance of the general ethos of the school, the attitudes of teachers and the role of parents.

'It's no good suspending children who bully. They should be isolated, given detentions or whatever. And teachers should look into whether parents are supporting the children in their attitudes. The school needs to talk to the parents.'

Kurtis Hall

'I was very open. My first year at [secondary] school we had to do these talks that showed everyone the kind of person you are and I got my foster mum to come in and I just said, 'Look, you've all got to know I'm in care, if you don't like it, you don't like it, if you do, you do, it's your problem not mine. And my mum came in and explained what foster care was, how it worked and why some children are in care. And they just understood, basically. But that's the kind of area I live in. People are very understanding. There's two children's homes in the area where I live and people are quite understanding at the school. But sometimes people have bad attitudes. One time, this kid in my class went completely nutty and the teacher said, 'Are you in foster care?' And I stood up and said, 'Why do you ask that?' And he said, 'Well, kids in care do that.' And I went, 'Excuse me?' And I went, 'I'm in care.' And his face, his jaw just dropped.'

Kay Connolly

Conclusion

This report has been finished just as yet another enquiry into the abuse of children within the child care system is published (the Waterhouse report into abuse in North Wales children's homes). It is clear that some fundamental, and detailed, questions need to be asked of the organisations whose role it is – on behalf of us all – to protect and promote the welfare of the most vulnerable children in our society. Those interviewed for this report have provided a starting point for those questions.

From what they told me, it seems clear that all services – the way they are funded, organised and what they do – should be measured against two criteria:

- Does this service promote and protect the human rights of children?
- Can this service be tailored to meet the needs of an individual child – even if these needs are different from the majority of the children who use the service?

The current body of research tells us quite a lot about what goes wrong for children in the care system. There is also some research, although not enough, on what works, usefully summarised in the Barnardo's series of that name (for example, Jackson and Thomas, 1999; Sellick and Thoburn, 1996). There has been less attention paid, however, to the barriers to change created by the care system itself. We know less about how the legislative framework, the organisation and funding of services, the training and recruitment of staff, the general social context get in the way of change – or how they can be used to promote change.

This report has attempted to start to address these two important questions. It has been written at a time of unprecedented government attention to what local authorities are doing to promote and protect the interests of children. This is also a time when the human rights agenda generally has come to the fore in terms of both general public awareness and political debate. There may, therefore, now be an opportunity to ensure that the human rights of children become central to what everyone, and anyone, does for looked after children in general, and each looked after child in particular.

Bibliography

Audit Commission (1999) **Getting the Best from Children's Services: Findings from the Joint Reviews of Social Services 1998/9**. Department of Health

Bains, Rav (1999) 'An equal service: How can Quality Protects be used to help looked after black and ethnic minority children?' **Community Care**, 28 January–3 February, Inside, p. 4

Baldry, Sally and Kemmis, John (1998) 'Research Note: What is it like to be looked after by a local authority?' **British Journal of Social Work**, 28, 129–136

Barn, Ravinder, Sinclair, Ruth and Ferdinand, Dionne (1997) **Acting on Principle: An examination of race and ethnicity in social services provision for children and families.** BAAF/CRE

Berridge, David (1997) **Foster Care: A research review**. The Stationery Office

Biehal, N and others (1995) **Moving On: Young people and leaving care schemes**. HMSO

British Agencies for Adoption and Fostering (1995) **See You Soon: Contact with children looked after by local authorities**. BAAF

Bullock, Roger, Little, Michael and Millham, Spencer (1993) **Residential Care for Children: A review of the research**. HMSO

The Children's Society (1997) **I'll Go First: The planning and review toolkit for use with children with disabilities**. The Children's Society

Daniel, Paul and Ivatts, John (1998) **Children and Social Policy**. Macmillan

Department of Health (1992) **Choosing With Care. Report of the Committee of Inquiry into the Selection,**

Development and Management of Staff in Children's Homes. HMSO

Department of Health (1999a) **Mapping Quality in Children's Services: An evaluation of local responses to the Quality Protects Programme. National overview report**. Department of Health.

Department of Health (1999b) **The Quality Protects Programme: Transforming children's services – 2000/01**, LAC (99) 33. Department of Health

Department of Health (1999c) **Social Services Performance 1998–99**. Department of Health

Department of Health (1999d) **Convention on the Rights of the Child: Second report to the UN Committee on the Rights of the Child by the United Kingdom**, Department of Health

Department of Health (1998a) **Caring for children away from home: Messages from research**. John Wiley and Sons

Department of Health (1998b) **Someone Else's Children: Inspections of planning and decision-making for children looked after and the safety of children looked after**. Department of Health

Department of Health (1998c) **Objectives for Social Services for Children**. Department of Health

Department of Health (1998d) **Quality Protects: Framework for action**. Department of Health

Department of Health and Local Government Association (1999) **Think Child! The councillor's guide to Quality Protects**, Department of Health

Fletcher-Campbell, Felicity (1997) **The Education of Children who are Looked After**. NFER

Gulbenkian Foundation (1993) **One Scandal Too Many: The case for comprehensive protection for children in all settings**. Gulbenkian Foundation

Hill, Malcolm (1997) 'What children and young people say they want from social services', **Research, Policy and Planning**, 15, 3, 17–27

Hills, Dione and Child, Camilla (1998) **Leadership in Residential Care: Evaluating qualification training**. Wiley

House of Commons Select Committee on Health (1998) **Children Looked After by Local Authorities, Vol 1: Report and Proceedings of the Committee**. The Stationery Office

Ince, Lynda (1998) **Making it Alone: A study of the care experiences of young black people**. British Agencies for Adoption and Fostering

Jackson, Sonia and Thomas, Nigel (1999) **On the Move Again? What works in creating stability for looked after children**. Barnardo's

London Borough of Newham (1999a) **Children Looked After: What it's like**. London Borough of Newham Social Services

London Borough of Newham (1999b) **Space for Us: Finding out what disabled children and young people think about their placements**. London Borough of Newham Social Services

Millham, S, Bullock, R and Hosie, K (1986) **Lost in Care**. Gower

Morris, Jenny (1998a) **Still Missing: Vol 1. The experiences of disabled children and young people living away from their families**. The Who Cares? Trust

Morris, Jenny (1998b) **Still Missing: Vol 2. Disabled Children and the Children Act**. The Who Cares? Trust

Parker, Roy A (1988) 'Residential care for children' in Sinclair, Ian ed. **Residential Care: The research reviewed**. National Institute for Social Work

Sellick, C and Thoburn, J (1996) **What Works in Family Placement?** Barnardo's

Shaw, Catherine (1998) **Remember my Messages: The experiences and views of 2000 children in public care in the UK**. The Who Cares? Trust

Sinclair, Ian and Gibbs, Ian (1998) **Children's Homes: A study in diversity**. John Wiley and Sons

Sinclair, Ruth and Grimshaw, Roger (1997) **Planning to Care: Regulation, procedure and practice under the Children Act 1989**. National Children's Bureau

Social Services Inspectorate (1993) **Corporate Parents: Inspection of residential child care services in 11 local authorities**. Department of Health

Social Services Inspectorate (1996) **For the Children's Sake: An SSI Inspection of Local Authority Adoption Services**. Department of Health

Social Services Inspectorate (1998a) **Removing Barriers for Disabled Children: Inspection of services to disabled children and their families**. Department of Health

Social Services Inspectorate (1998b) **Someone Else's Children: Inspections of planning and decision-making for children looked after and the safety of children looked after**. Department of Health

Social Services Inspectorate (1999a) **Getting Family Support Right: Inspection of the delivery of family support services – Key messages for practitioners and first-line managers**. Department of Health

Social Services Inspectorate (1999b) **Getting Family Support Right: Inspection of the delivery of family support services**. Department of Health

Social Services Inspectorate (1999c) **Modern Social Services: A commitment to improve. The 8th Annual Report of the Chief Inspector of Social Services**. Department of Health

Social Services Inspectorate (1999d) **Planning to Deliver: Inspection of children's services planning**. Department of Health

Social Services Inspectorate and Office for Standards in Education (1995) **The Education of Children who are Looked After by Local Authorities**. Department of Health and Ofsted

Support Force for Children's Residential Care (1995) **Code of Practice for the Employment of Residential Care Workers**. Department of Health

Thomas, Nigel and O'Kane, Claire (1998) **Children and Decision Making: A summary report**. University of Wales, Swansea

Triangle (1999a) **Tomorrow I Go: What you told us about Dorset Road – Young people's views about a residential respite service**. Triangle, Unit 310, 91 Western Road, Brighton, East Sussex BN1 2NW

Triangle (1999b) **Listening on all Channels: Consulting with disabled children and young people**. Triangle

United Nations **Convention on the Rights of the Child**. Adopted by the General Assembly of the United Nations on 20 November 1989.

United Nations (UN) Joint Working Party on Foster Care (1999) **Report and Recommendations**. National Foster Care Association

United Nations Children's Fund (UNICEF) (1998) **Implementation Handbook for the Convention on the Rights of the Child**. UNICEF

Utting, Sir William (1991) **Children in the Public Care: A review of residential child care**. HMSO

Utting, Sir William (1997) **People Like Us: The report of the review of the safeguards for children living away from home**. Department of Health and The Welsh Office

Voice for the Child in Care (1998) **Shout to be Heard: Stories from young people in care**. Voice for the Child in Care

Waterhouse, R (2000) **Lost in Care. Report of the tribunal of inquiry into the abuse of children in care in the former county council areas of Gwynedd and Clwyd since 1974**. The Stationery Office

Waterhouse, S (1997) **The Organisation of Fostering Services**. NFCA

Wheal, A and Sinclair, R (1995) **It's Your Meeting: A guide to help young people get the most from their reviews**. National Children's Bureau

Whittaker, Dorothy, Archer, Lesley and Hicks, Leslie (1997) **Working in Children's Homes: Challenges and complexities**. John Wiley & Sons

The Who Cares? Trust (1998) **The Social Care of Children: A summary of current issues and concerns in the social care of children and young people**. (Paper prepared for Joseph Rowntree Foundation consultation event). The Who Cares? Trust

Index

adoption 26
attitudes to children 1–3
Audit Commission 36

Barnardo's Family Placement Services 50
Best Value Framework 31, 36–37
Birmingham City Council 38
black children vii, 10, 15, 44
bullying 55–56
business efficiency 5

care system vii
children, attitudes to 1–3
Children Act (1989) vii, 5, 17, 30
children in care, attitudes to 3–4, 28–30
children with disabilities see disabled children
children's attitudes 18–19
Children's Family Trust 50
children's homes see residential care
children's needs 7–9, 15
children's relationships 19
children's rights 4–5, 14, 17, 30, 32–34
Children's Services Plans 40–41
child/social worker relationship 48–49
communication impairments 31
communication skills 13–14
consultation, with children v, vii, 2–3, 17, 30–32, 35–36, 41

continuity of care 8–9, 50

DfEE guidance 55
disabled children vii, 10, 16–18, 31, 44

education vii, 6, 20–23, 53–56
    support for 'looked-after' children 22–23, 53–55
    see also schools
education departments 23–24
emotional development vii
equal opportunities 16
ethnic minority children see minority ethnic

families, contact with vii
foster care 7–9, 25, 38
foster carers 9–10, 42–44, 49
fragmentation of care 6–7
funding 8–9, 37–39

'good parents' 6, 35
government policy v–vi, 26–27

House of Commons Select Committee on Health 11, 38, 41

inspections 16, 34, 36
inter-agency working 23–24, 34, 52
inter-personal skills 13–14
interviews vi, 41

joint working 23–24, 34, 52

local authorities, responsibilities
    34–35
Looked After Children
    documentation 12, 52–53, 55

management, of social services 4–5,
    45–46
minority ethnic children vii, 10,
    15–16, 43–44
monitoring 36–37
moral framework 5
multidisciplinary working 23–24, 34,
    52

National Care Standards
    Commission 36
National Priorities Guidance 55
needs-led approach v, 8, 51

outcomes vi–vii, 19

parenting 1–2, 6, 35
partnership with parents 25
Performance Assessment
    Framework 37
Personal Education Plans 55
placement, continuity of vii, 51
placements 8–9, 17, 19, 36, 38, 42
Pro-Teen 50

Quality Protects 24, 31, 35, 37–38,
    53–54

research 24–26
residential care 11, 41–42
    strategy 40
residential care places 10–11
residential care workers 14–15, 45–47
    support 39–40

respite, for foster carers 43
review meetings 17

Safeguards Review 39
schools 21
    pastoral care 20
    response to 'looked-after' children
        20, 53–56
    see also education
service-led approach 7–9, 51
services, flexibility 50–52
Social Exclusion Unit 24
social services 23–24
    attitudes 4–5
    management 4–5, 45–46
    responsibilities 6–7, 36, 44–47
Social Services Inspectorate 36
social worker/child relationship
    48–49
social workers 12–14, 36, 38–39
    attributes 13, 46–47
staff development 44–47
Support Force for Children's
    Residential Care 40
support workers 38

teachers 21–22, 29, 55–56
    see also schools
'Think Child' 35
training v, 14, 31, 42, 45–47

UN Convention on the Rights of the
    Child 5, 17, 30, 32–33
Utting Review 10–11

Voice for the Child in Care 8

Warner Report 40
Waterhouse Report 57
Who Cares? Trust survey vii–viii